Mel Bay's **PRIVATE L.**

Rock/Fusion
Improvising

taught by...

Carl Filipiak

ONLINE AUDIO

1	Minor Family Chords	21	D Dorian Triads	41	G Diminished Scale (Whole-step/Half-step)	61	D flat and E flat triads
2	Fourth Chords	22	D Dorian in Sevenths	42	G Half-step/Whole-step scale (no extra charge)	62	C and D major triads
3	More Fourth Chords	23	Phrase using Sevenths	43	Minor thirds moving in scale steps	63	G and D flat triads
4	Fifths	24	Longer Phrase	44	Minor thirds	64	Giant Steps Changes
5	More Fifth Chords	25	F and G Triads	45	More minor thirds	65	Line 1
6	Seconds and Sevenths	26	Groups of Four	46	One more	66	Line 2
7	Fourths, Seconds and Thirds	27	On the "and"	47	Wide intervals	67	Line 3
8	D Minor Pentatonic Scale	28	Passing tone	48	More wide intervals	68	Jazz Waltz
9	Combined Positions	29	Combined Positions Ascending	49	Triads	69	Samba
10	Added Ninth	30	Lines using fourths	50	More triads	70	D minor Funk
11	More Combined Positions	31	More fourth lines	51	C Melodic Minor	71	5/4
12	Fourth Intervals	32	Fifths moving in thirds	52	Line 1	72	6/8
13	Fourth Intervals at 12th Fret	33	Fifths moving in fourths	53	Line 2	73	7/8
14	D Major Pentatonic Flat 3rd	34	More fifths in fourths	54	Imaginary Chords	74	17/8 (8 and 1/2)
15	Koto Vibe	35	Suspended Chords	55	Group of 5	75	Slash Chords
16	D Diminished Combo	36	Sus Blues	56	3 plus 5	76	Rhythm Changes
17	Pentatonic 1/2 steps	37	G Half-step/Whole-step scale	57	Group of seven	77	G Suspended Blues
18	Fourths and Fifths	38	Dominant sounds	58	7 plus 9	78	C Minor Blues
19	Root, 2nd, 3rd and 5th of scale	39	G13♭9 and G7♯9♯11	59	Triad pairs	79	Hotel Reàl
20	Scale degree motifs	40	Intervallic Chords	60	G and A augmented triads		

To Access the Online Audio Go To:
www.melbay.com/20408BCDEB

© 2004 BY Mel Bay PUBLICATIONS, INC., PACIFIC, MO 63069.
ALL RIGHTS RESERVED. INTERNATIONAL COPYRIGHT SECURED. B.M.I. MADE AND PRINTED IN U.S.A.
No part of this publication may be reproduced in whole or in part, or stored in a retrieval system, or transmitted in any form
or by any means, electronic, mechanical, photocopy, recording, or otherwise, without written permission of the publisher.

Visit us on the Web at www.melbay.com — E-mail us at email@melbay.com

ROCK/FUSION IMPROVISING

introduction

Hello, I'm Carl Filipiak and welcome to my book, Private Lessons/Rock Fusion Guitar. A lot of great music evolved in the late 60's when Miles Davis introduced elements of rock to the jazz world and created fusion. Since then, other genres have had a tremendous impact on jazz. Artists borrowing from funk, Latin, Indian and beyond were creating some incredible and exciting music! Mahavishnu Orchestra, Return to Forever, Weather Report, Pat Metheny, John Scofield and Tribal Tech, are just a few of the groups that have taken their music to new places–places that are diverse and yet have their roots in jazz.

This book will shed some light on many of the concepts unique to fusion. Applying these ideas to your playing will not only help you with the tunes I've included in the play-along CD, but with other fusion and jazz tunes as well! I've tried to make this book as "rock-friendly" as I can, and as long as you're familiar with the basics of rock and blues, you'll be able to relate to most of the examples. However, if you are fairly well versed in jazz, you will find it easier to understand.

The information I've chosen for this project comes from my experience as a private instructor and is in response to some of the questions I am most frequently asked. It is my wish that I not only try to give some answers, but share my enthusiasm and respect for all styles of creative music.

Carl Filipiak has earned critical acclaim as one of today's most dynamic jazz guitarists. *Jazziz Magazine* has included him among a renowned list of guitar players in their nominations for "New Fusion Blood," and *JazzTimes* calls him "a dazzlingly versatile guitarist."

He has recorded and performed with many of the industry's finest musicians including Dennis Chambers, Victor Wooten, and Grammy nominee Bob Berg. His six independent recordings on Geometric Records have garnered him reviews in such prestigious publications as *20th Century Guitar, Billboard, Guitar Player, Guitar World, Jazziz* and *JazzTimes*. Turner Broadcasting and NBC Sports have featured Carl's music in various televised events including the Olympics.

Carl performs at various festivals and venues along the east coast and is currently recording his latest CD. He is also actively involved in music education, has released his own instructional guitar video "Use What You Got!" and is an endorser and clinician for Fender Guitars and Dean Markley Strings.

Selected Discography (available from the author)

Blue Entrance - *featuring Dennis Chambers on drums*–Geometric Records

Right on Time - *featuring Bob Berg and Dennis Chambers*–Geometric Records

Hotel Reàl - *featuring Bob Berg, Will Calhoun, Gary Thomas and Dennis Chambers*–Geometric Records

Peripheral Vision - *featuring Dennis Chambers, compilation and bonus tracks*–Geometric Records

Looking Forward Looking Back - *featuring Dennis Chambers*–Geometric Records

Carl Filipiak
P.O. Box 18922
Baltimore, MD. 21206
website: www.carlfilipiak.com
email: carfil@aol.com

Special thanks to Royce Faddis for really getting this together. To my wife Irene, and the band members: Paul Soroka, John Thomakos and Steve Zerlin…can't thank you guys enough! Thanks to Doug Chandler, Dave Hunter, Mike Johnson, Dennis Chambers and John Grant. And to wherever guitars and electricity come from…eternal thanks!

Table of Contents

Intro/Acknowledgements 2
Harmony 4
Intervallic Harmony 5
Melody 7
Motifs 12
Triads 13
Sequences 14
Intervals 15
Suspended Chords 17
Dominant Sounds Derived from the Diminished Scale 18
I Only Know Four Scales 21
The Melodic Minor Scale 24
Imaginary Chords and Other Cool Stuff 26
Triad Pairs and Odd Note Groupings 27-28
Giant Steps Changes 30
Odd Time Signatures and Assorted Grooves 31
Short List of Slash Chords 33
Song Forms 34

harmony

I'll start with some ways to generate chords by constructing them in intervals other than thirds. Many tunes in fusion (and jazz) have a section to solo over based on one chord. I've chosen D minor 7th as an example. Not only can you play D minor 7th, but D minor 9, D minor 11, and D minor 13 as well. The upper tensions do not effect the basic quality of the chord, which is minor. These chords are in the minor family and are commonly used in many musical situations. I'll also refer to them as "root based" chords, since there is a root on the 6th or 5th strings.

CD Track 1

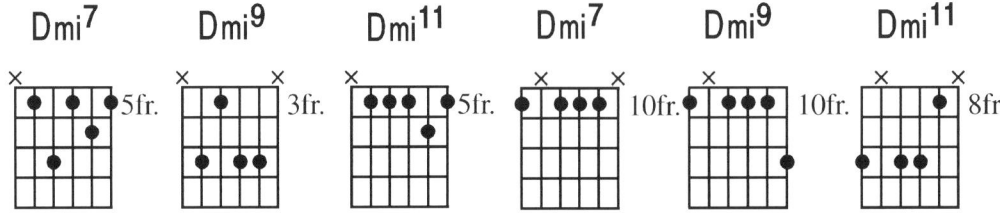

It is now necessary to know the scale or mode that D minor 7th is generated from. This is because chords are scales and scales are chords! More precisely said, scales generate harmony (chords), and chords imply scales. Check out what happens when we use the D Dorian mode. The notes are **D E F G A B C D**. Starting with D and moving in thirds, it's easy to see that the notes D, F and A when played harmonically produce a D minor triad. Keep on imposing thirds and now you'll see how the minor 7th, 9th, 11th and 13th chords are constructed. It's sometimes easier to see this when the scale is written in two octaves.

D	E	F	G	A	B	C	D	E	F	G	A	B	C	D
R		♭3		5		♭7		9			11		13	

It won't hurt to know what the upper tensions in chords are, and an easy way to do this is to know the 2nd, 4th, and 6th degree of the scale. Find those notes and just add 7. The 2nd is the 9th, in this case E. The 4th is the 11th, which is the note G, and the 13th is the same note as the 6th, B. Now that you know how we arrived at the chords in example 1, let's construct chords based on intervals other than thirds.

Hotel Reàl Guitar Solo

CD Track 79 *(from the CD "Hotel Reàl" by Carl Filipiak)*

Let's add another 5th. Why not?!

CD Track 5 ⇨

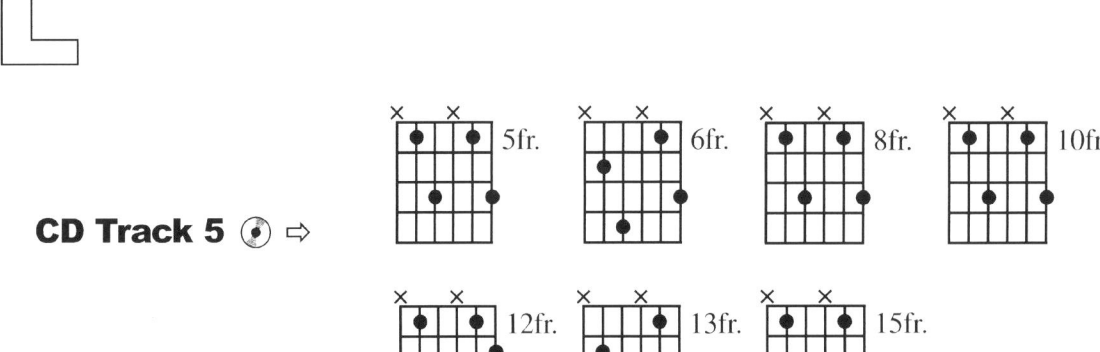

Now that you can see and hear the melodic potential of these voicings, let's choose some sounds based on different intervals. Here are some that I like to use a lot and hopefully trying these out will help you to create your own. These are built from D Dorian using seconds and sevenths.

CD Track 6 ⇨

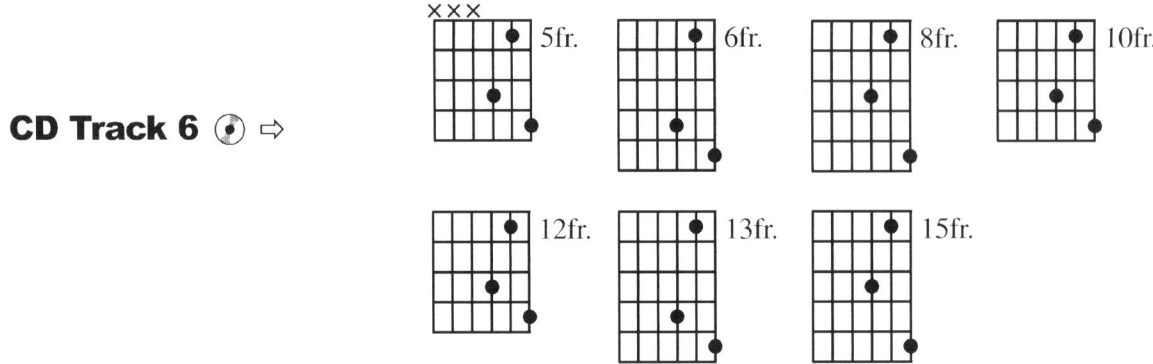

These are built by using fourths, seconds and thirds. Some of these require a little stretching, but are worth the effort!

CD Track 7 ⇨

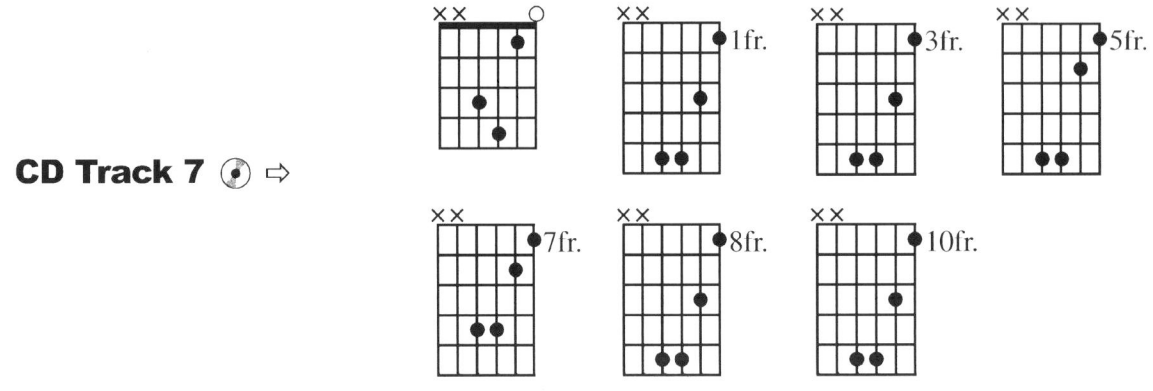

I could keep going but by now I'm sure you have the idea and I hope I've inspired you to come up with some of your own voicings. Continue with 6ths, 7ths, etc., and the odds are in your favor to come up with something cool! These structures also work for any mode in the key of C major, since D Dorian is derived from that scale.

Here's a quick overview to help you create your own new chords.

1. Choose a scale / mode.
2. Pick two intervals at random.
3. Construct on every note of scale.
4. Use melodically by hearing the top voice.
5. Smaller intervals imply closeness and wider intervals imply space.

melody

pentatonics

Finally! Let's play over some of the previous chord patterns. These ideas will sound great over D Dorian. Useful when playing over an extended modal vamp found in many fusion and jazz tunes. I'll start by using the minor pentatonic scale because of its familiarity. Here's something that rock players getting into fusion can start doing. Take a look at these common scale patterns.

CD Track 8

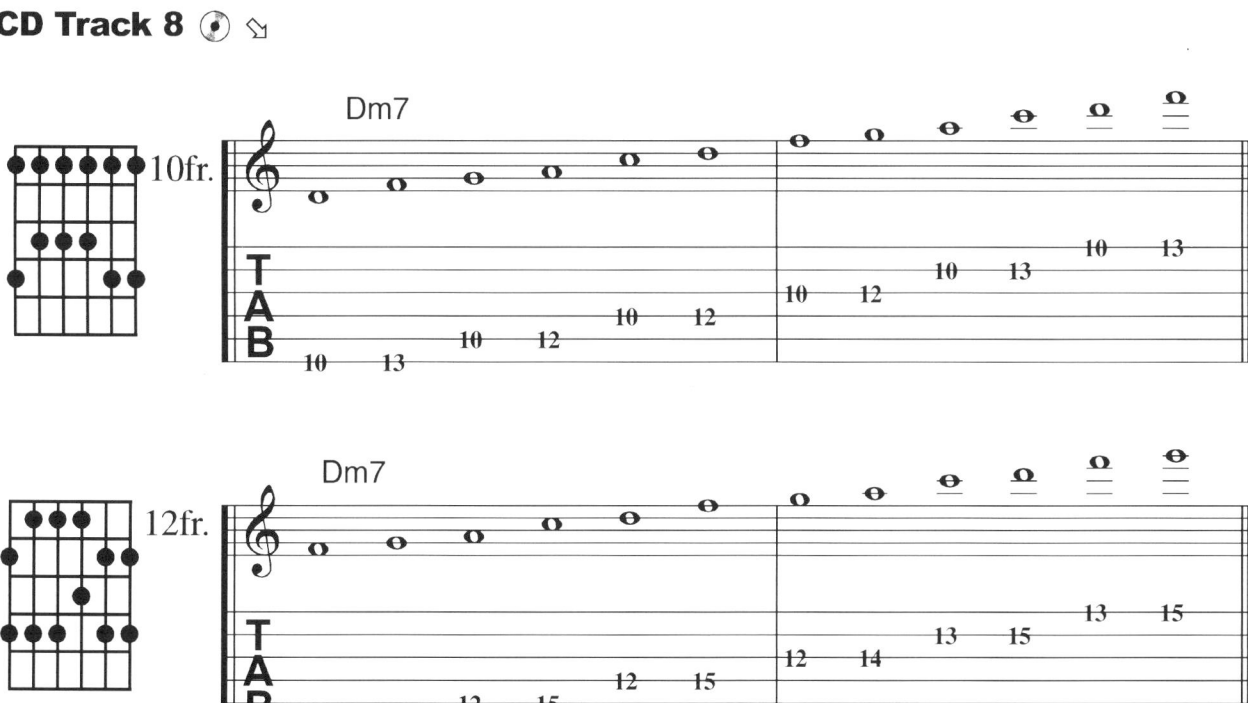

Look at them combined. With a slight adjustment in fingering, some cool sounds can be played. This combining of positions now lends itself to wider intervals of a 4th on the same string, as well as unison notes on adjacent strings. The stretching will be worth it.

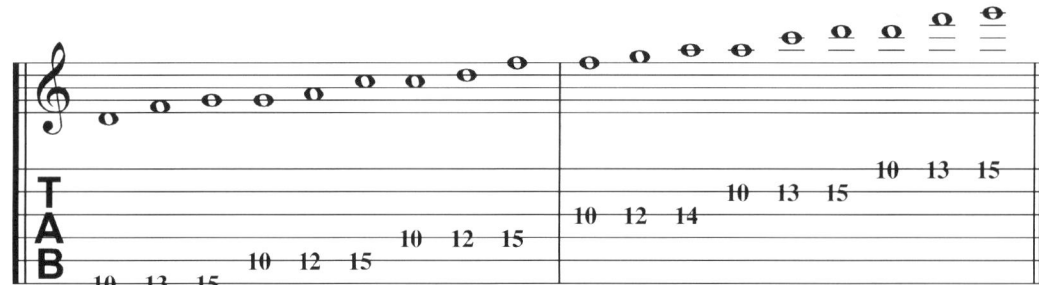

CD Track 9

Try adding a note from the scale. In this case the 2nd or 9th, E.

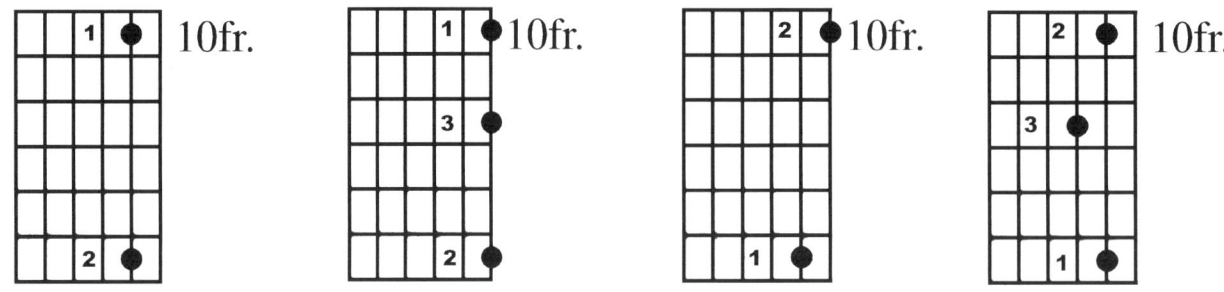

8

CD Track 10 🎧

Check out these two D minor pentatonic scales.

CD Track 11 🎧

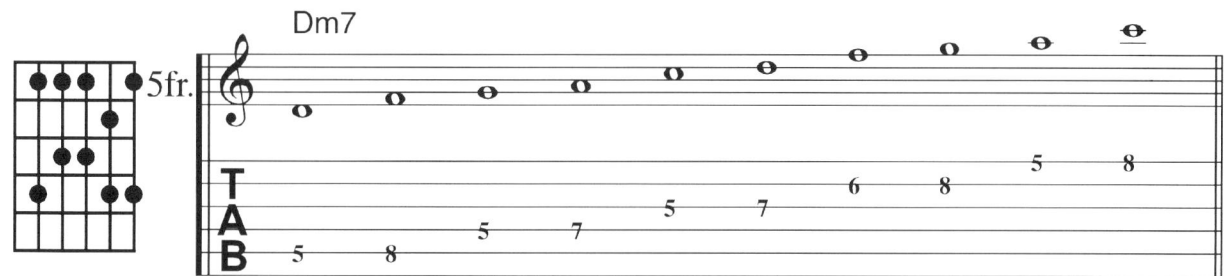

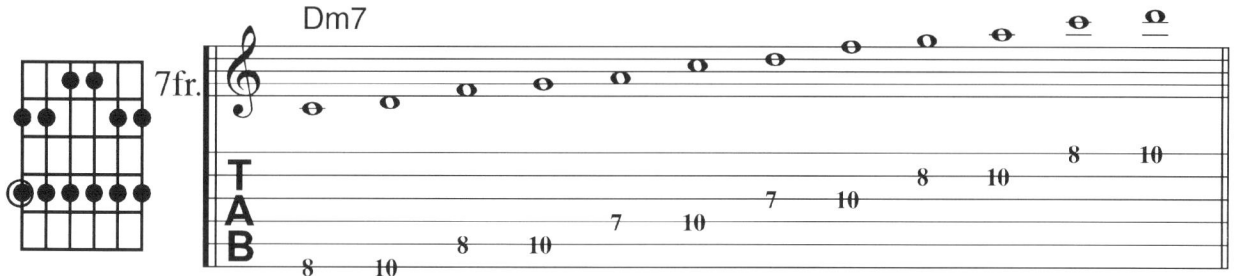

Now Combine:

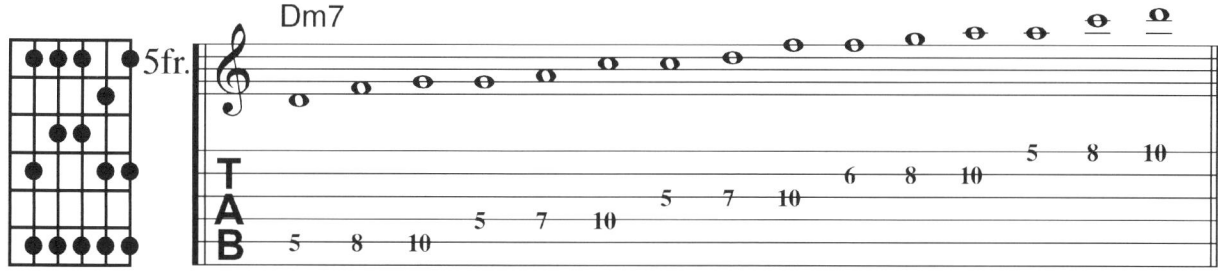

Here are some cool ways to plays 4ths.

CD Track 12

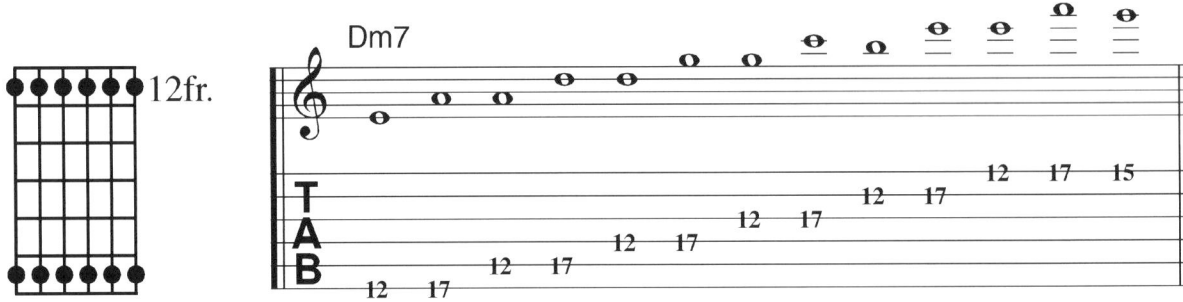

Try the same thing starting on the 12th fret.

CD Track 13

Try playing these notes D, E, F, A and B. You could think of this as an altered pentatonic scale (D major pentatonic flat 3rd) or notes derived from D Dorian.

CD Track 14

Try playing this scale with a koto technique for a Japanese vibe. Think East meets West or Eric Johnson. Not recommended on your blues gig!

CD Track 15

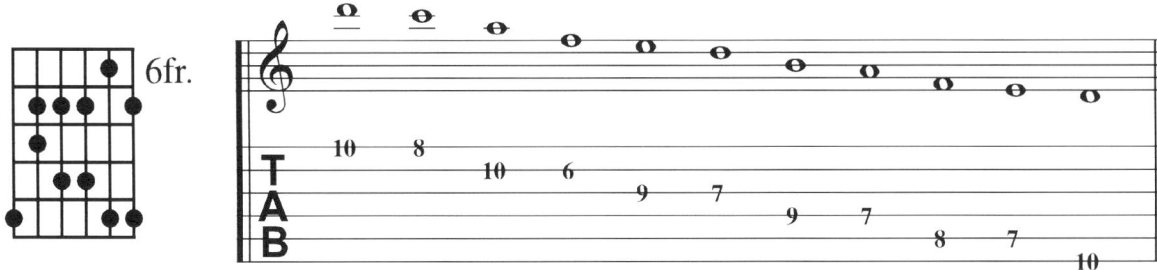

Let's get a little further out by borrowing some notes from a **D diminished 7th chord.**

D	F	A♭	B
R	♭3	♭5	6th

CD Track 16

And speaking of playing out, one of the easiest ways to create some tension in your playing is to play a half step above or below the key you're in. This example uses a D minor pentatonic scale and E♭ minor pentatonic scale played against a D minor 7th chord.

CD Track 17

I've used the more familiar minor pentatonic scale in the 10th position, but don't let that stop you from playing it elsewhere.

motifs

Try this short musical phrase on different notes of the scale. It's based on intervals of a 4th and 5th.

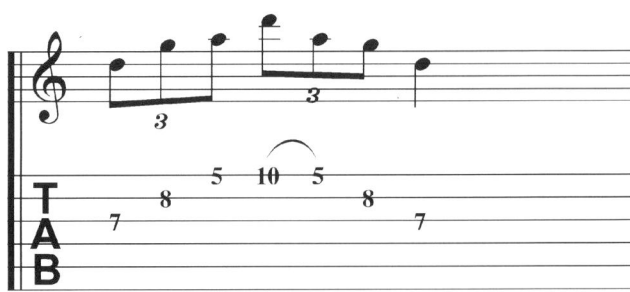

Try it in two octaves.

CD Track 18

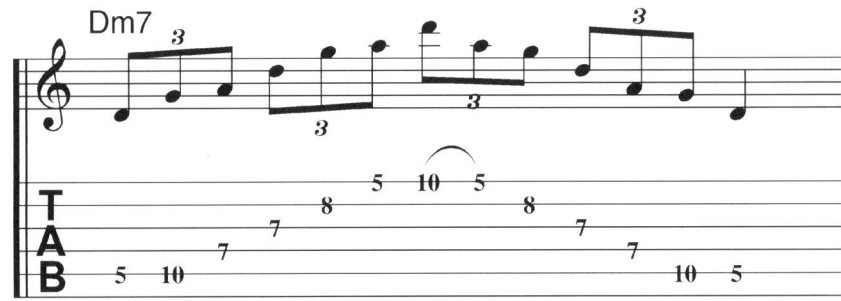

Here's another one using the Root, 2nd, 3rd and 5th degree of the scale.

CD Track 19

Once again, only this time start on different notes of the scale.

CD Track 20

12

triad pairs

Two triads found within a scale can imply the sound of many chords. For D-7 use an F and G major triads.

CD Track 59

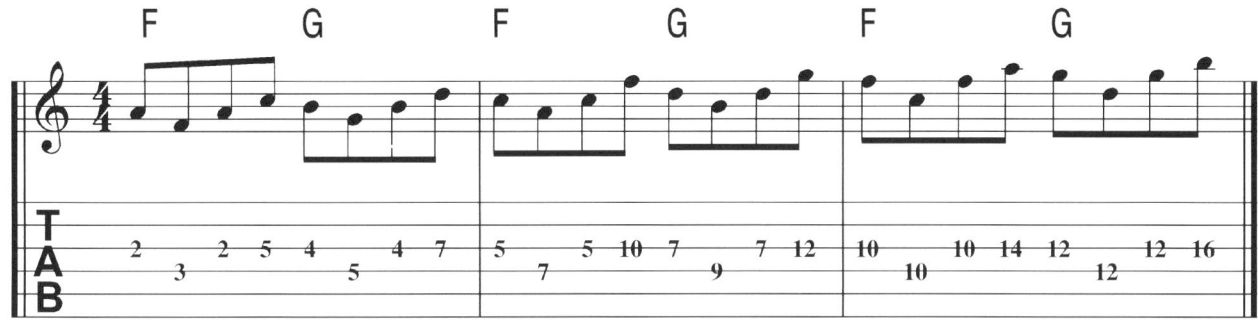

For G Lydian ♭7 sounds use G and A triads or G and A Augmented triads.

CD Track 60

For a G Altered Dominant Chord use D♭ and E♭ triads.

CD Track 61

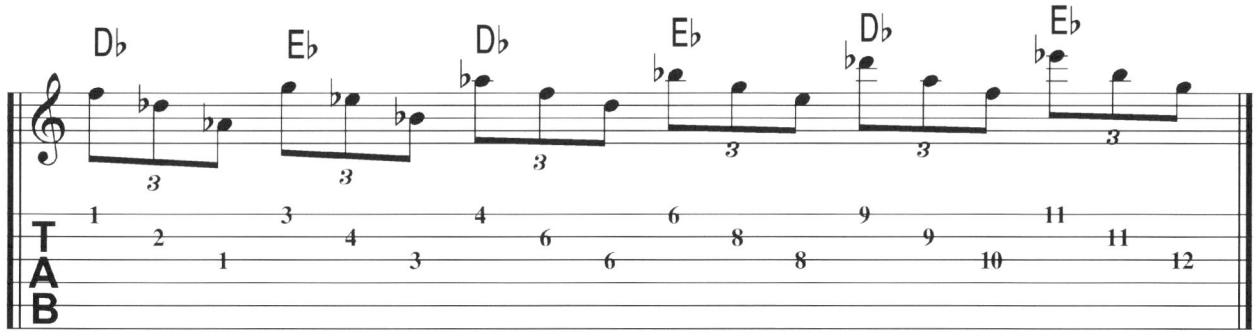

CD Track 24

Here's one using an F triad and G triad.

CD Track 25

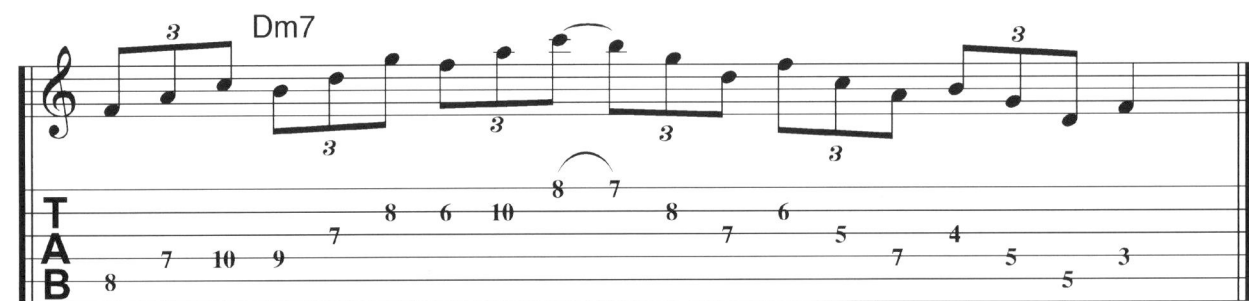

sequences

We've all played or heard scales played in groups of four.

CD Track 26

To make it sound less like an exercise, start it on the "and" of one.

CD Track 27

...or start with a passing tone.

CD Track 28

Try this sequence based on a pentatonic scale utilizing two positions.

CD Track 29

intervals

Here are some lines using 4ths.

CD Track 30

CD Track 31

Try fifths moving in 3rds.

CD Track 32

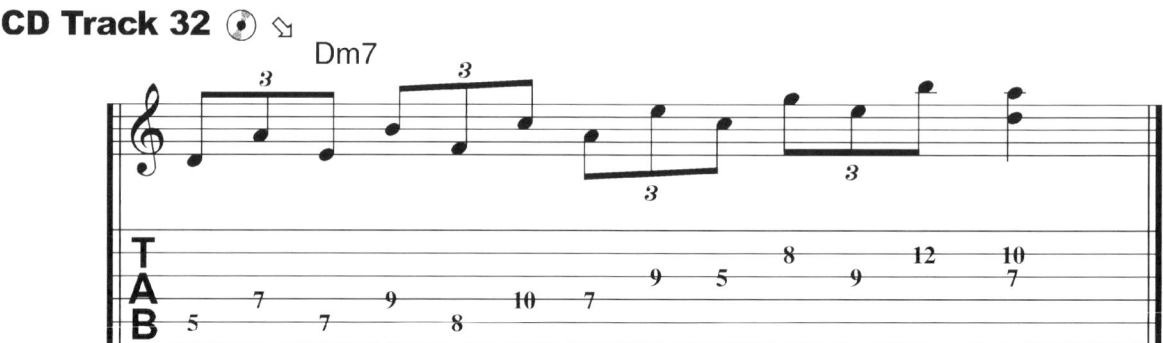

Fifths moving in 4ths.

CD Track 33

CD Track 34

looking back:

So far, the examples that we used contain only notes of the D Dorian mode. (The exceptions were example 16 and 17). Here's a review of the concepts we have covered and how to start multiplying their uses.

1. Try these same ideas over dominant (Mixolydian) and Lydian modes. Play each scale in intervals of 3rds, 4ths, 5ths, etc.
2. Eventually be familiar with all modes of C major. Once again, they are D Dorian, E Phrygian, F Lydian, G Mixolydian, A Aeolian and B Locrian.
3. Know the triads and seventh chords in all modes.
4. Try sequences in groups of three, four, five notes and beyond. (See you in a few years!)

Just kidding! A way to make this seem less daunting is to realize that all the information we learned and worked on in D Dorian will sound great over G Mixolydian and F Lydian as well. All notes have a melodic and harmonic relationship with each other, since they share the same parent scale, C major. If you don't get this right away, don't worry, eventually you will. For now just try some of these same ideas over a G sus Chord or an F 6/9 #11 chord and you'll hear what I mean. Jazz guitarists frequently use this concept of relating Dorian ideas to other sounds quite frequently. It's a reminder that great fusion players have a strong link to jazz.

suspended chords

Suspended chords are constructed with the Root, 4th, 5th, and flat 7th of a scale. Available tensions in the suspended family include the 9th, 11th(4th), and 13th. A G Sus chord contains the notes G, C, D, and F. The 9th is A, the 11th(4th) is C, and the 13th is E. A suspended chord can also be described as a dominant chord with the 3rd raised. Here are a few examples of suspended chords with roots on the 6th or 5th strings.

CD Track 35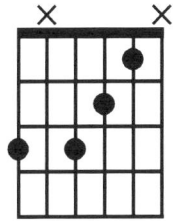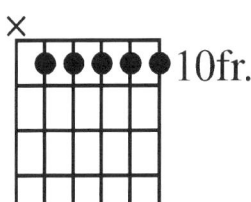

y introduction to this sound was the tune "Maiden Voyage" by Herbie Hancock. Try using this on a basic 12-bar blues, playing sus chords instead of dominant chords.

CD Track 36

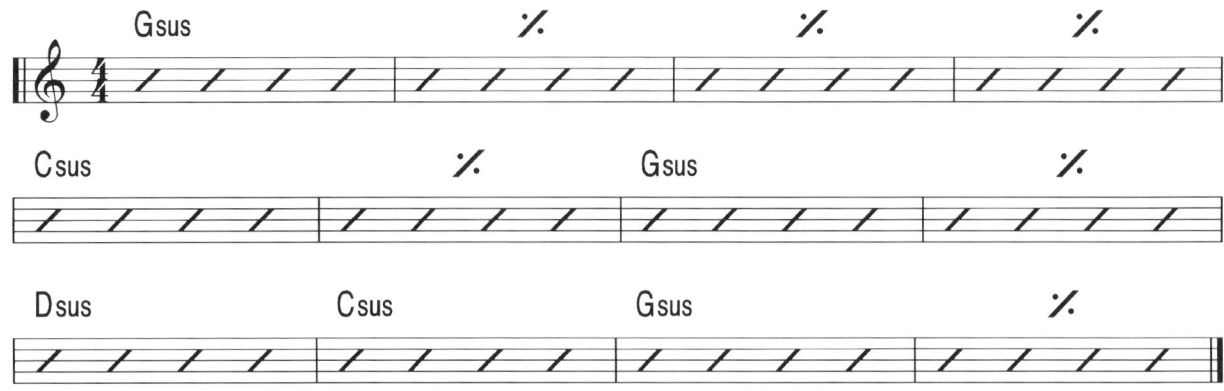

Tips for soloing: Play G Mixolydian over G Sus. It's the 5th degree of C major or a G major scale with a flatted seventh. Or try playing a Dorian mode a fifth above the root. D Dorian sounds great over G Sus and with a few adjustments all the melodic examples we just went through will sound fine. Use your ears and this concept of minor conversion will enhance your ability to solo over different chord types. Don't forget to play G Dorian over C Sus and A Dorian over D Sus when soloing over a G Suspended Blues!

dominant sounds derived from the diminished scale

These symmetric sounds will accept a blues scale as well as the half-step/whole-step diminished scale that they are constructed from.

They are heard and used in many jazz tunes.
The G half-step/whole-step scale sounds great over these chords. Here is the scale: G, A♭, B♭, B, C♯, D, E, F, and G.

CD Track 37

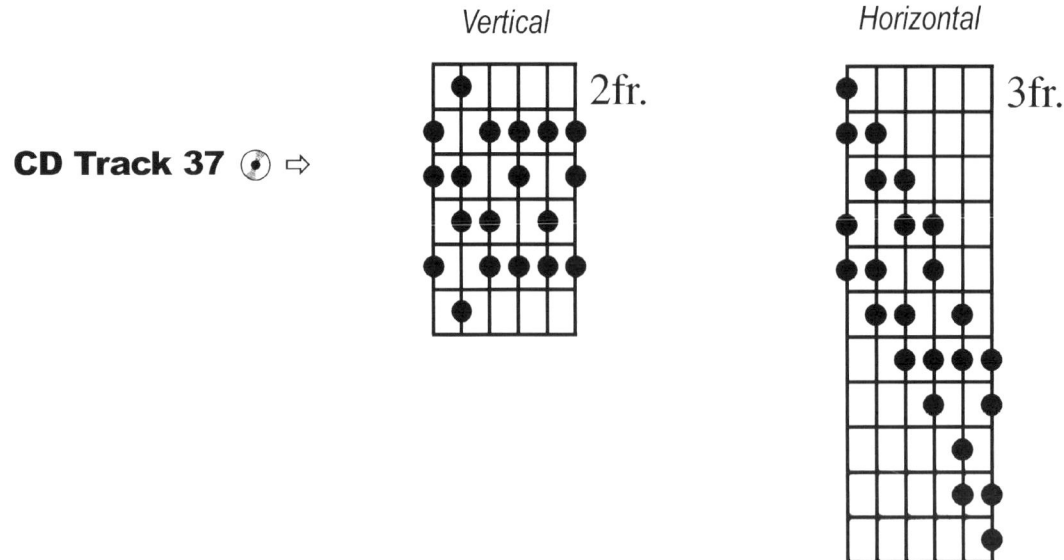

Here are some chords that this scale generates: G7, G7♭9, G7♯9, G7♭5, and G13.

CD Track 38

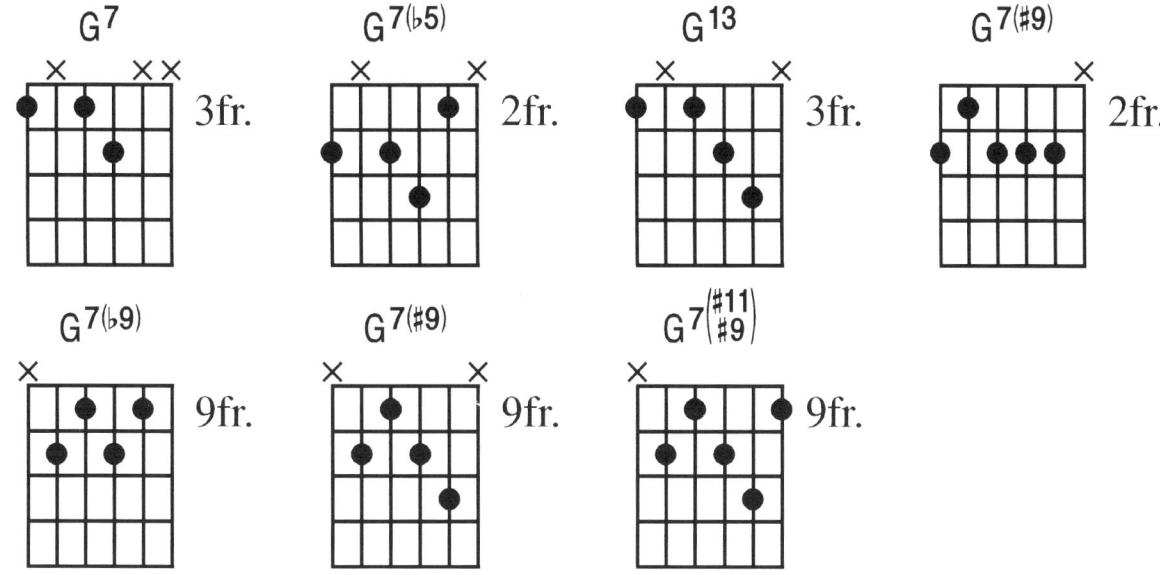

Here are the triads within the scale: G, B♭, D♭, and E major triads as well as G minor, B♭ minor, C♯ minor and E minor triads.

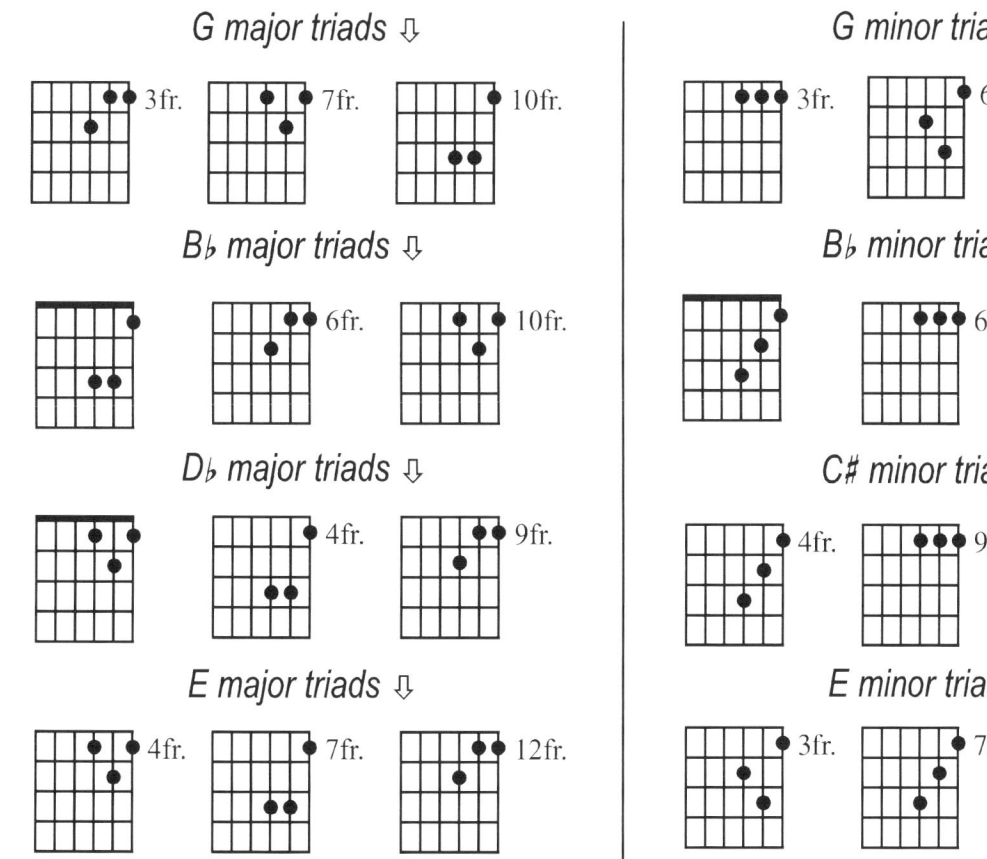

13♭9 and G7♯9♯11 are two root position chords you should know and can also be thought of as an E triad over a G7 chord and B♭ minor over G7 respectively.

CD Track 39

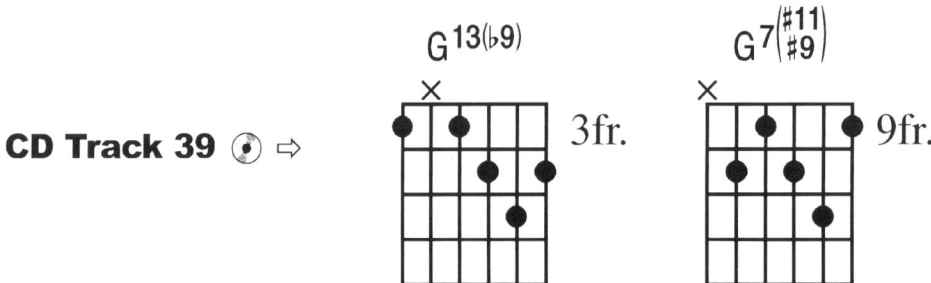

Here are some cool chords based on intervals of that scale. Since the scale is symmetric, all chords are movable in minor 3rds, (3 frets)!

CD Track 40

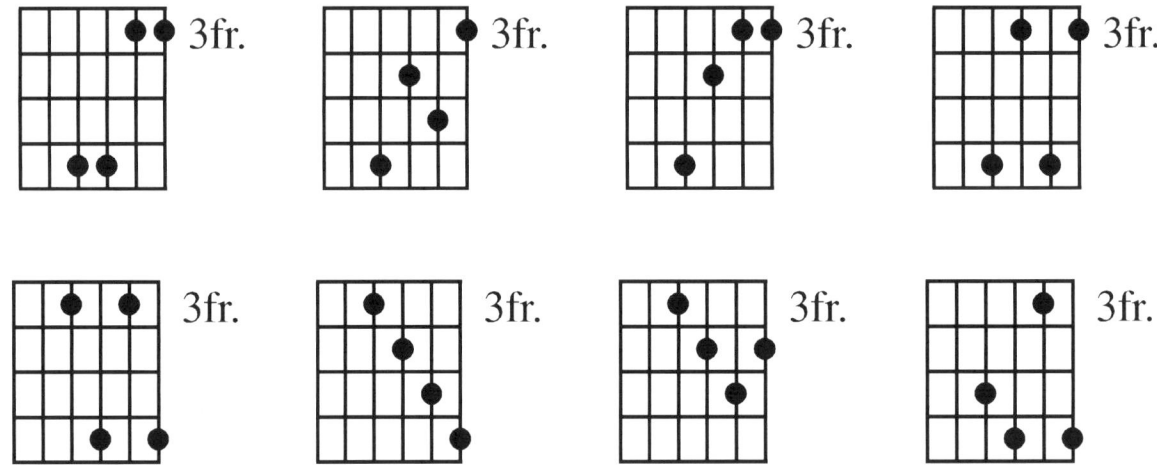

looking forward:

Coming up in the section on soloing, you'll see how a lot of the lines will be based on triadic shapes used in some of the chords you just learned. By being more familiar with this concept, you'll not only see where things are coming from, but you'll be able to create your own solos as well.

looking back:

Even though you won't hear these chords in blues or rock tunes, licks derived from a G minor pentatonic scale and/or blues scale will sound great over them. It's a great way to get started and later we'll add a few more ideas.

I only know four scales

There are quite a few scales that are used extensively in fusion and one way to learn them is to know their parent scales inside and out. A C Major scale produces seven modes. Multiply that by 12 and you have 84 different scales! Call me old fashioned, but I'd rather reduce the amount of information I need when improvising. I only use these four scales when playing: the major scale, jazz melodic minor, diminished and the whole-tone scale. Let's check out the diminished scale.

Here's a brief look at the construction of a diminished scale. When used against a diminished chord, start with intervals of a whole step then a half. For example play this scale over a G dim7 chord.

G	A	B♭	C	D♭	E♭	E	F♯	G
R	W	1/2	W	1/2	W	1/2	W	1/2

However when used against a Dominant sound, start with intervals of a half step then a whole step.

G	A♭	B♭	B	C♯	D	E	F	G
R	1/2	W	1/2	W	1/2	W	1/2	W

Against a G7 chord this scale produces tensions of ♭9 as well as ♯9, ♯11 and natural 13.

H ere are some ideas for soloing. Use the chords referred to in the section "Dominant Sounds Derived From The Diminished Scale."

Minor 3rds moving in scale steps.

CD Track 43

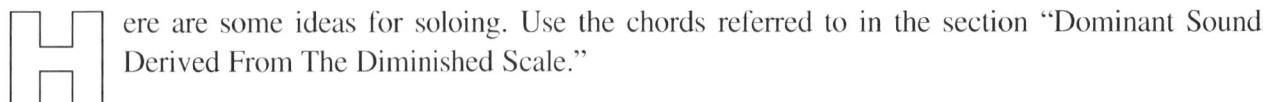

Patterns moving in minor 3rds.

CD Track 44

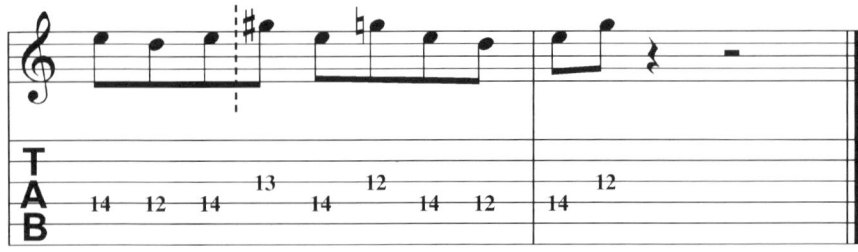

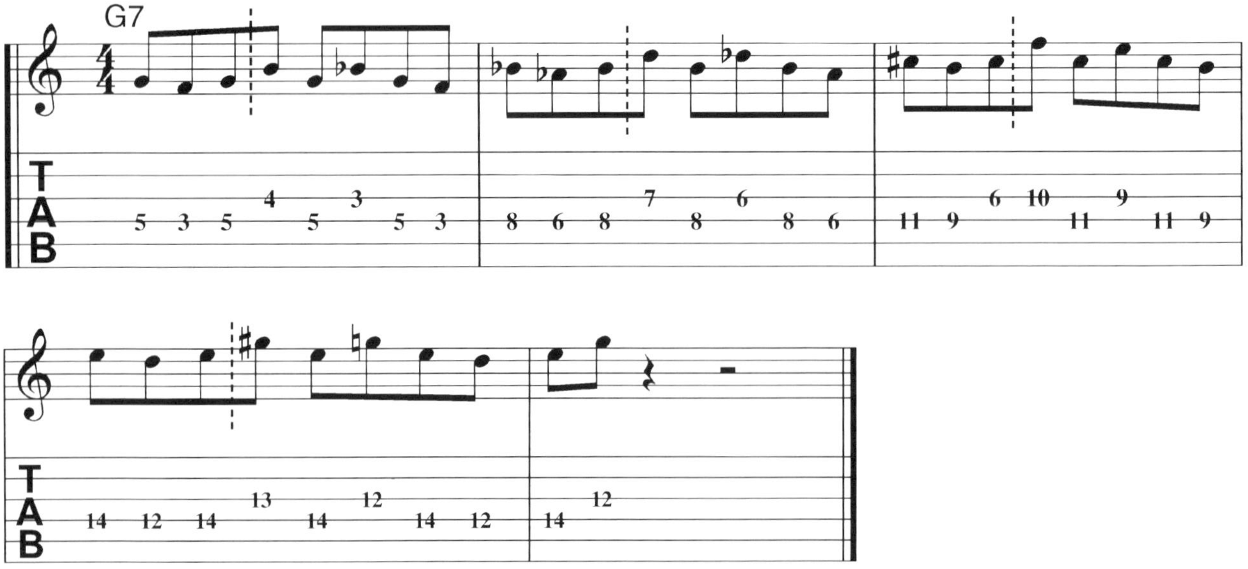

CD Track 45

CD Track 46

Wide intervals.

CD Track 47

move in minor thirds →

CD Track 48

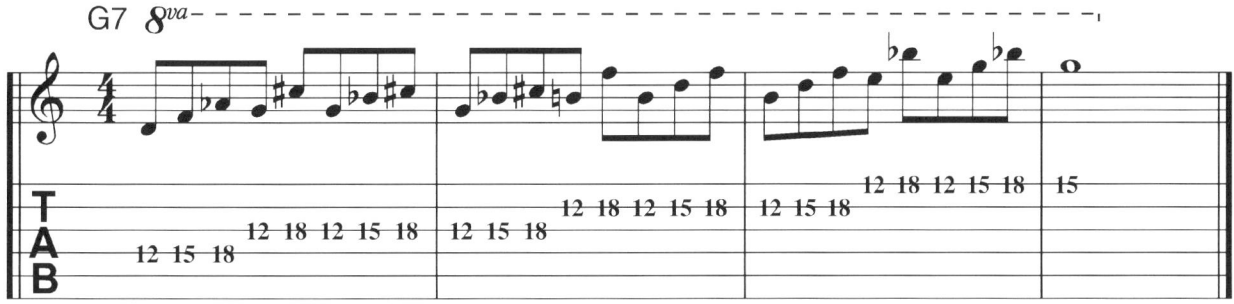

triads

CD Track 49

move in minor thirds →

CD Track 50

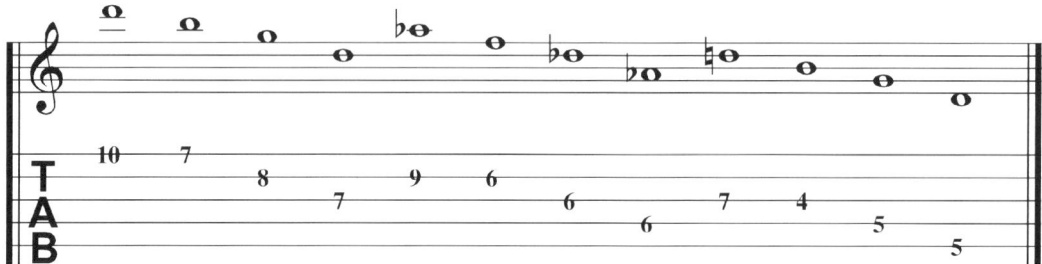

Overview

1. Since the scale is symmetric, find a short phrase and move it up or down the fretboard in minor 3rd's (three frets).
2. Triads are G Major, B♭ major, D♭ major and E major as well as minor.
3. Not responsible for loss of wages due to use on weddings, bar-mitzvahs, etc!

the melodic minor scale

The melodic minor scale I'll be using is also called the **jazz melodic minor scale.**

Here are the notes:

C	D	E♭	F	G	A	B	C
R	W	1/2	W	W	W	W	1/2

CD Track 51

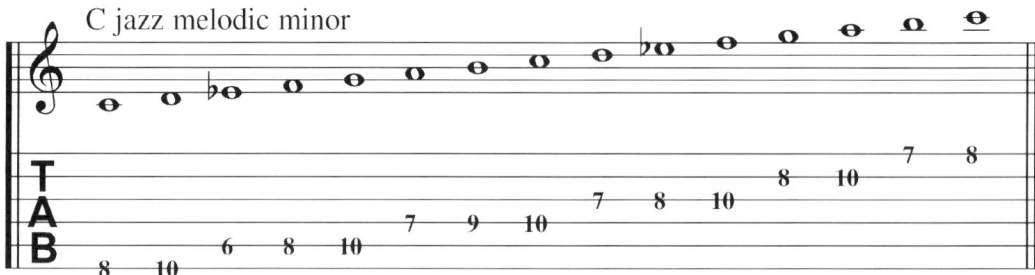

It ascends and descends using the same notes. It can also be thought of as a C major scale with a flatted third. Changing one note of a scale that you already know will help you to visualize new patterns on the fretboard instantly. It is also a parent scale of seven scales/modes. Two of those used in fusion and jazz tunes are Lydian ♭7 and the altered dominant scale.

The following examples work over all three with little alteration. Try playing them over one of these chord vamps first, as well as play them over a C Dorian sound to add some tension. We'll talk more about superimposing scales over chords later. Chords that best define the sound of C melodic minor are: Cmi6, Cmi(Maj7), and Cmi(Maj9).

Here are some lines to try.

CD Track 52

Here's how we can multiply the application of these lines.

Try the examples over an F9#11 chord. The 4th degree of a Melodic Minor scale is Lydian b7. Also play them over a B7altered dominant chord. The 7th degree of a melodic minor scale is an altered dominant scale. There are 7 different modes of the melodic minor and these are very useful. Here are some lines to try.

CD Track 53

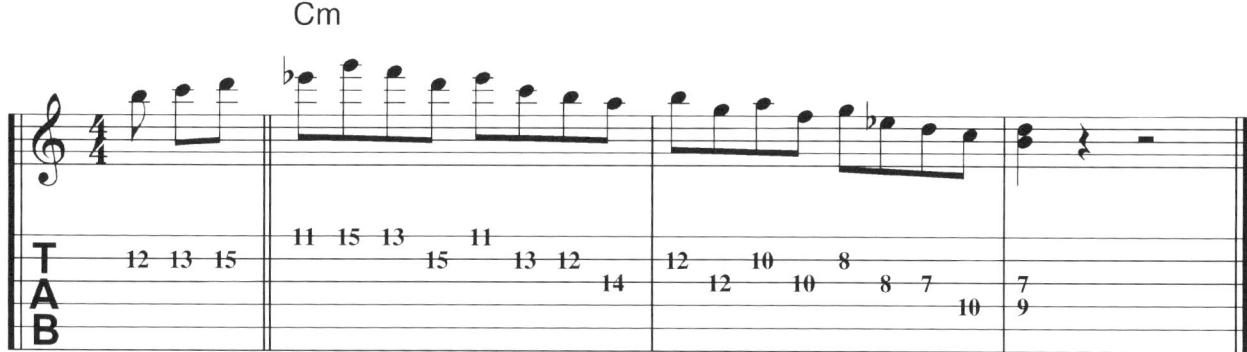

Looking Back:

1. The jazz melodic minor scale ascends and descends using the same notes.

2. A major scale with a flatted third = the jazz melodic minor scale.

3. Changing one note of a scale that you already know will help you to visualize new patterns on the fretboard instantly.

4. The fourth degree of a melodic minor scale is a Lydian b7 scale, and the seventh degree is an altered dominant scale.

imaginary chords and some other cool stuff!

In this section I'd like to talk briefly about imaginary chords, altered pentatonics, scalar interchange, odd note groupings, interchangeable 5th's and 7th's, "Giant Steps" changes and triad pairs. These are ways to play some really cool sounds that fall outside the boundaries of chord/scales.

Try this to start. Over a D Dorian extended vamp, add these chords:

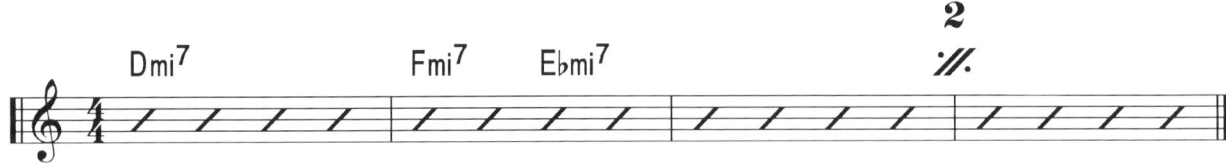

Now solo over them even though they are not being played!

CD Track 54

You can choose chord motion in any interval you like as long as you return back to Dmi7. It can also be thought of as chord over chord, but I think you'll get the idea of why they're called imaginary chords. Chords that imply a strong V to I relationship may be the easiest to hear at first. What makes this work is the symmetry of the line. It overrides the fact that some of the notes do not reflect the sound of a Dmi7th chord. Not recommended on a traditional blues gig!

odd note groupings

By phrasing in odd numbers, our lines will now be displaced over the bar line. Try these out and you'll hear what I mean.

Group of 5

CD Track 55

Group of 3 + 5

CD Track 56

(Play on all sets of strings.)

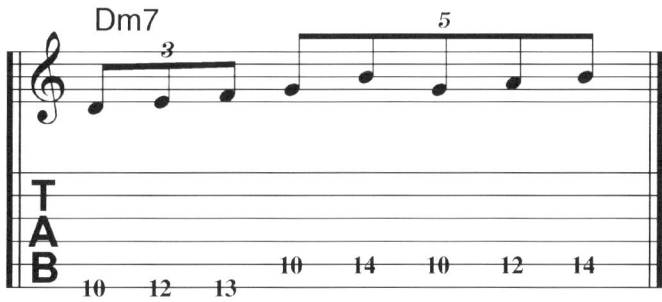

Group of 7

CD Track 57

Group of 7+9

CD Track 58

triad pairs

Two triads found within a scale can imply the sound of many chords. For D-7 use an F and G major triads.

CD Track 59

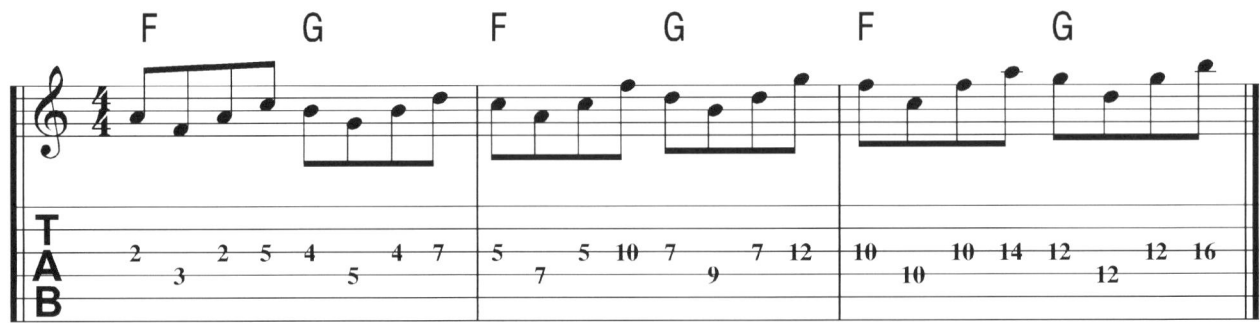

For G Lydian ♭7 sounds use G and A triads or G and A Augmented triads.

CD Track 60

For a G Altered Dominant Chord use D♭ and E♭ triads.

CD Track 61

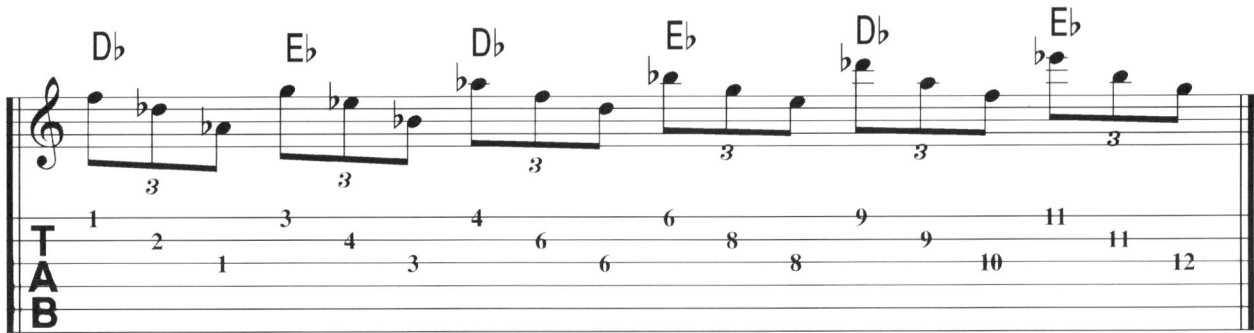

For C Lydian use C and D Major triads.

CD Track 62

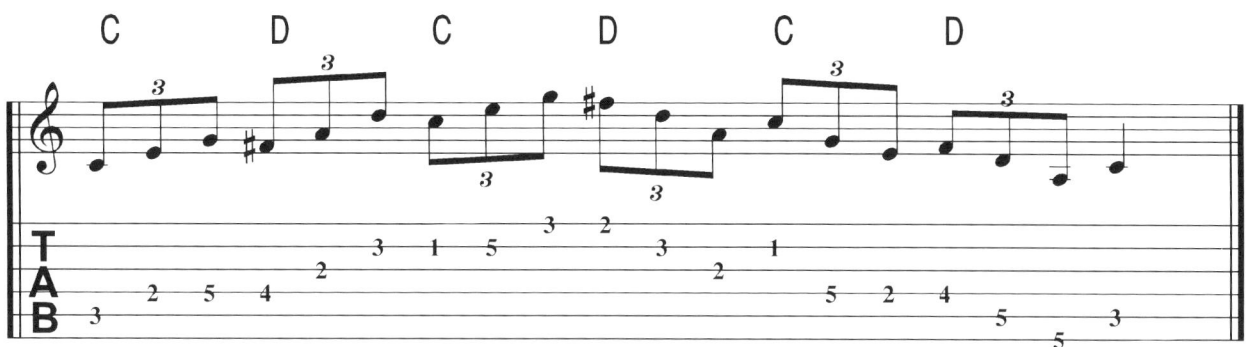

Over a G13♭9 chord try triads a flatted 5th apart.

CD Track 63

Looking Back:

1. For major Lydian, use the triad built on the root and a whole step above.

2. For minor 7th use triads built from the minor 3rd and 4th degrees.

3. For Lydian ♭7 use triads built on the root and a whole step above. You can also use an augmented triad a whole step above.

4. For altered dominant use triads built from the flatted 5th and raised 5th.

5. For 13th ♭9 chords use triads built from the root and a flatted 5th above the root. You can also move those ideas in minor thirds.

giant steps changes

 heck out this chord sequence based on the well-known Coltrane tune, "Giant Steps." I'll transpose it in G.

CD Track 64

This pattern of chords moving up a minor third and then down a fifth eventually returns home. Play some lines over these changes while soloing over a static G dominant chord.

CD Track 65

CD Track 66

CD Track 67

30

The symmetry of the chord changes holds this together for you, even though some of the notes against G could be considered "out." This is a great way to get acquainted with one of the most challenging songs to improvise over. It will also get you beyond the more inside way of playing using chord scales.

odd time signatures and assorted grooves

Fusion definitely has its share of tunes in odd time signatures, and one way to get acquainted with them would be to start with 3/4 time. The reason is that odd times can be expressed as a combination of and odd number (3) plus an even number. 5/4 can now be played as a jazz waltz plus two quarter notes. This is a fairly common way to divide five quarter notes in one measure. It's simply 3 plus 2. The song, "Take Five" is an example of this. The example on the CD in 5/4 is also divided into 3 plus 2. The example in seven is divided into 4 plus 3. The example in six can be heard as two 3's or a bar of 4 simultaneously to suggest a more polyrhythmic approach. Also very useful and common are various Latin and Brazilian rhythms. While that can be an entire subject in itself, you can get quite a bit of mileage out of Track 69. Last but not least 17/8 or 8 and a half! One way to count this is seven quarter notes and three eighth notes. John Wubbenhorst, Steve Zerlin and Sandip Burman introduced me to this Indian rhythm, they are masters of that genre and I'm not! However, I thought a funk version of that time signature would sound cool, and was glad to experience and share a real lesson in the spirit of music.

3/4 –Jazz Waltz
CD Track 68

4/4 –Samba, Bossa, Latin
CD Track 69

4/4 –Funky D minor
CD Track 70

5/4
CD Track 71

6/8 – 4 against 6 feel
CD Track 72

7/8 – divided 4 + 3
CD Track 73

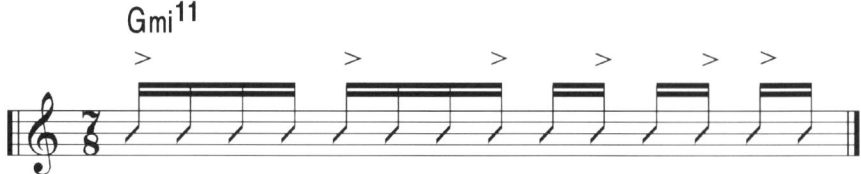

17/8 – divided 4 + 4 & 1/2
CD Track 74

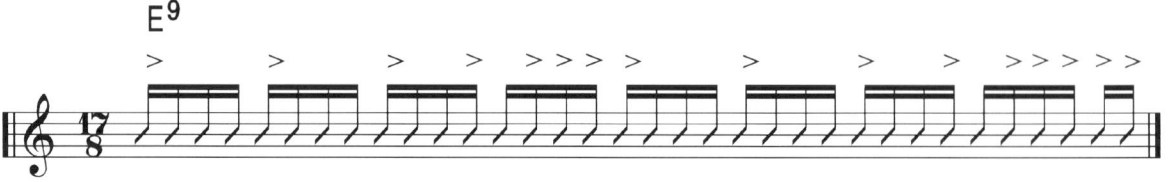

1. Odd plus even = odd

2. Jazz has been influenced by other rhythms as far back as Charlie Parker and Dizzy Gillespie.

3. Check out a couple tunes on the latest Jeff Beck CD's that are in odd time signatures. *Blast from the East* (Who Else -Epic) is in 15/8 and could be heard as a bar of 7/8 and a bar of 4/4. The tune *Earthquake* (You Had It Coming–Epic) is in 11/8.

4. I finally used some different chords in my examples to get away from D minor for a while!

the short list of slash chords

Try to get familiar with some of these sounds, as they'll be used when we (finally!) play some tunes in the Song Form Section. I've chosen some that best imply major, minor and dominant chord sounds. I presume they'll be more familiar to a jazz guitarist than a rock or blues player, but don't let that keep you from hearing their usefulness.

CD Track 75

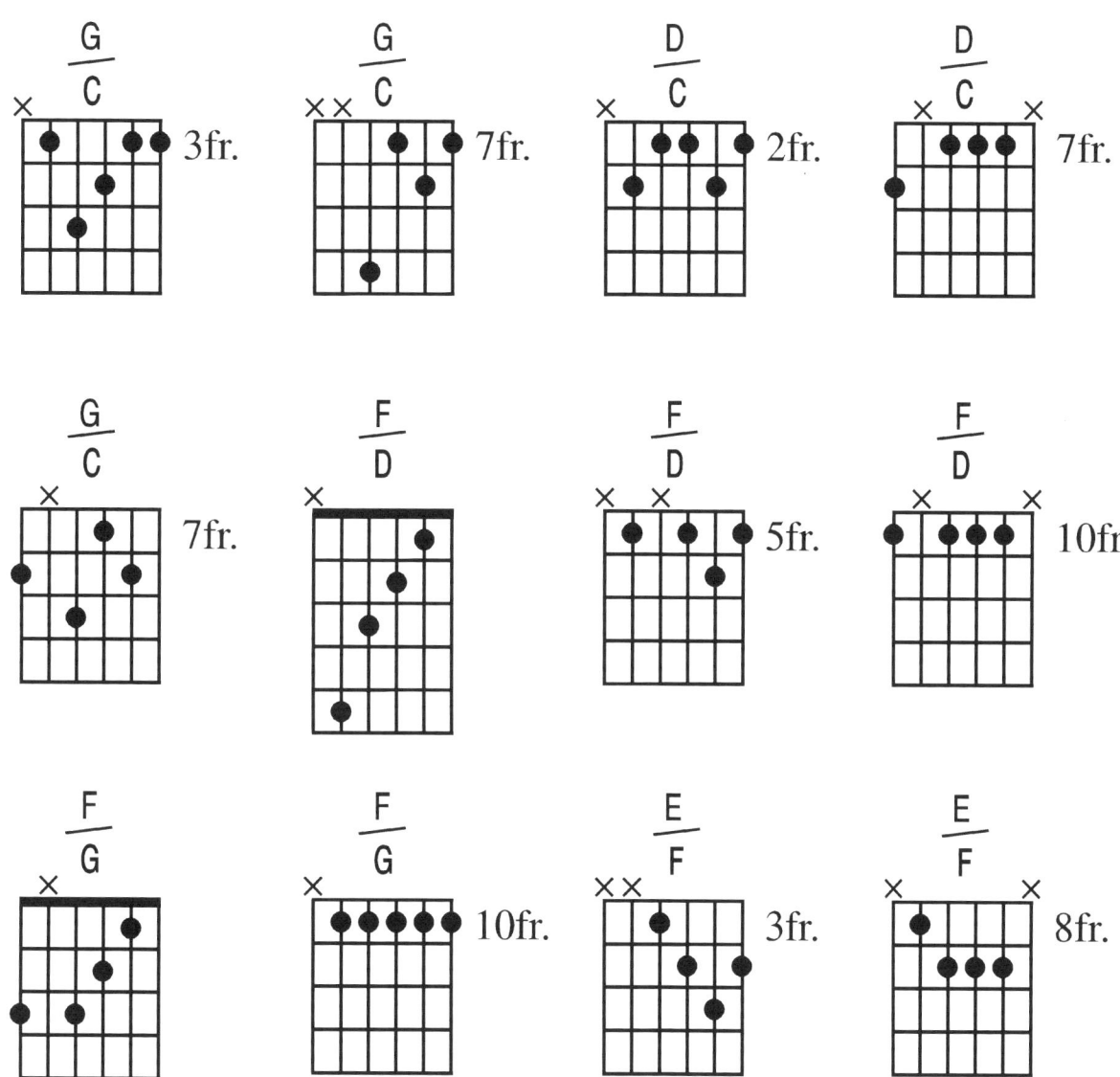

song forms

Fusion tunes borrow song forms commonly associated with jazz and are sometimes altered to create new sounds. These are included for you to play along with:

CD Track 76

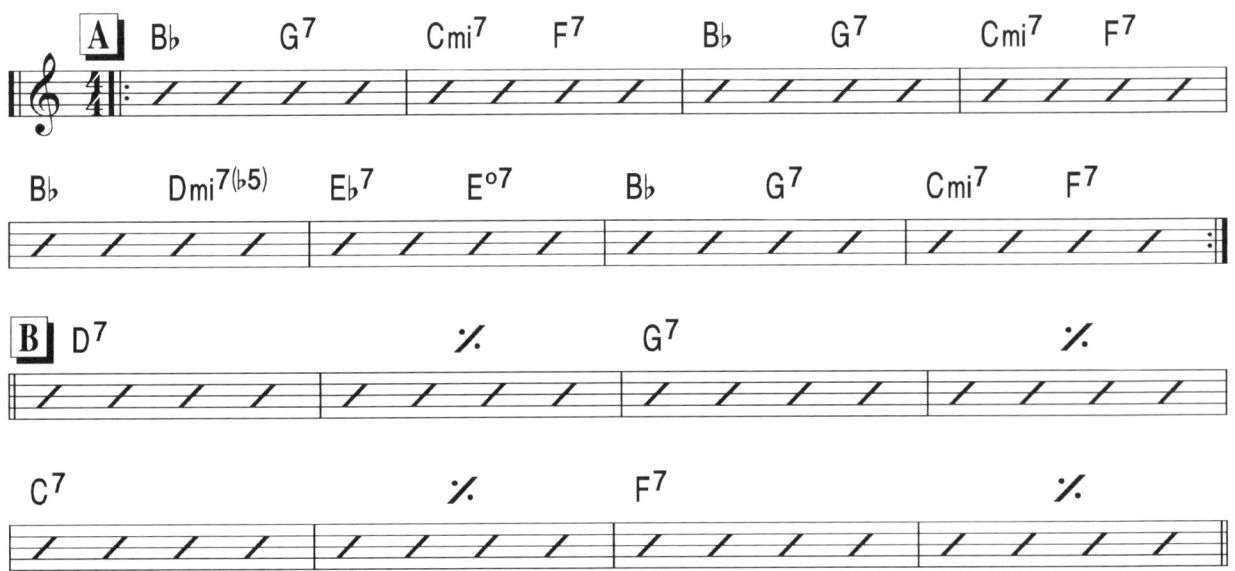

Rhythm Changes

Form: A A B A

CD Track 77

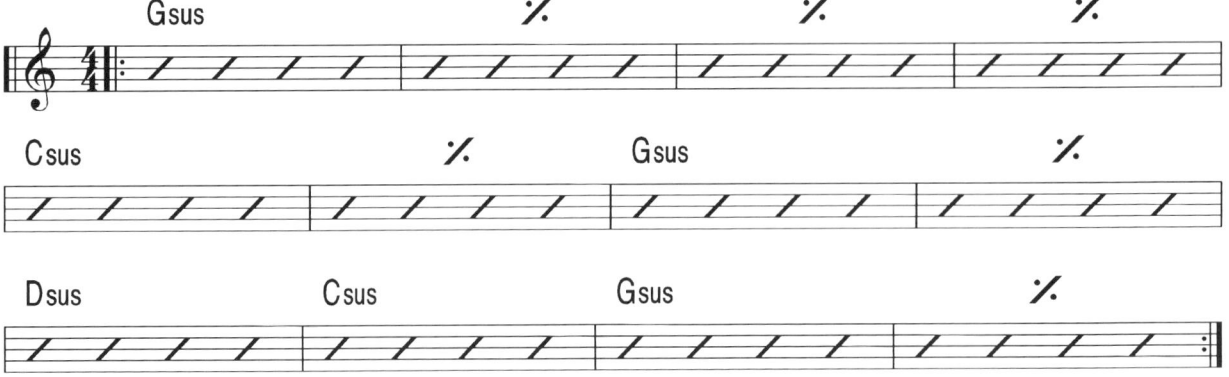

G Suspended Blues

CD Track 78

C Minor Blues

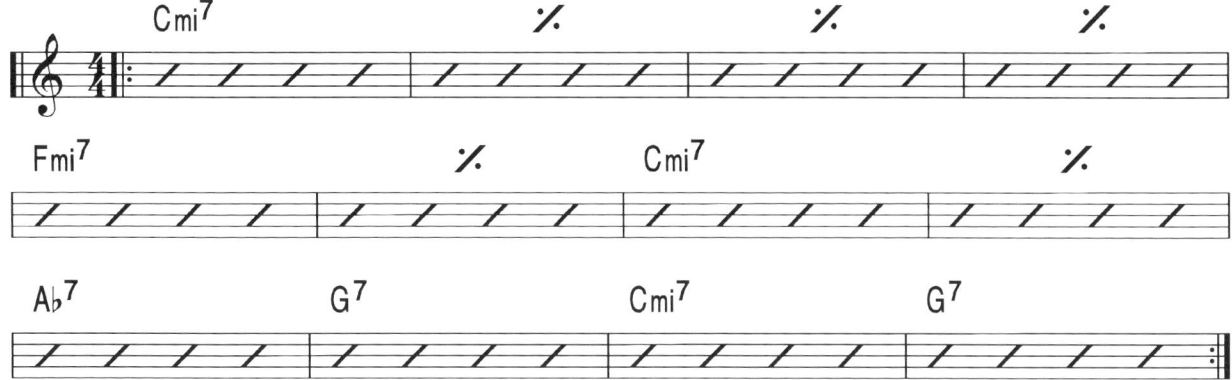

Minor blues changes are used for the solo section on the title track of Mike Stern's CD *Play (Atlantic)*. Check out the Tribal Tech tune "Susie's Dingsbums" (*Reality Check*). It's loosely based on rhythm changes. So are the tunes "Flat Out" by John Scofield (*Flat Out*-Gramavision) and "Lumpy" (*Give and Take*- Atlantic) by Mike Stern.

Standards found in the Real Book are also used in fusion tunes. On the CD *Flat Out* by John Scofield, the song "Softly" is based on a popular standard "Softly, as in a Morning Sunrise." Another example would be on Mike Stern's CD, *Play*. The tune "Outta Town" is based on the standard, "Have You Met Miss Jones."

The following example comes from one of my recordings, *Hotel Reàl* (Geometric Records) and uses the chord changes from Autumn Leaves to solo over.

CD Track 79

Hotel Reàl Solo Changes

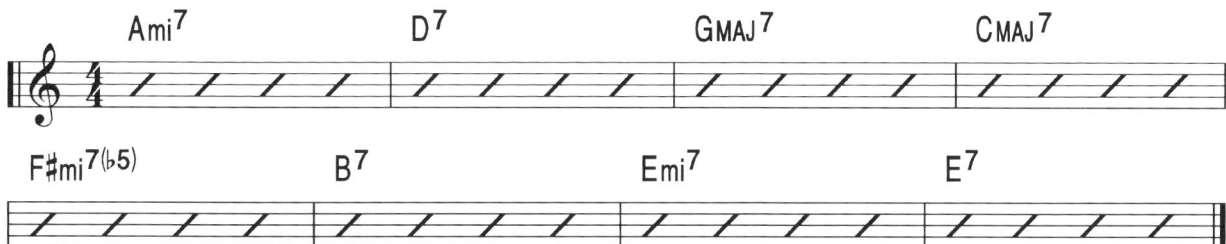

Hotel Reàl pg. 2

Hotel Reàl pg. 3

Hotel Reàl pg. 5

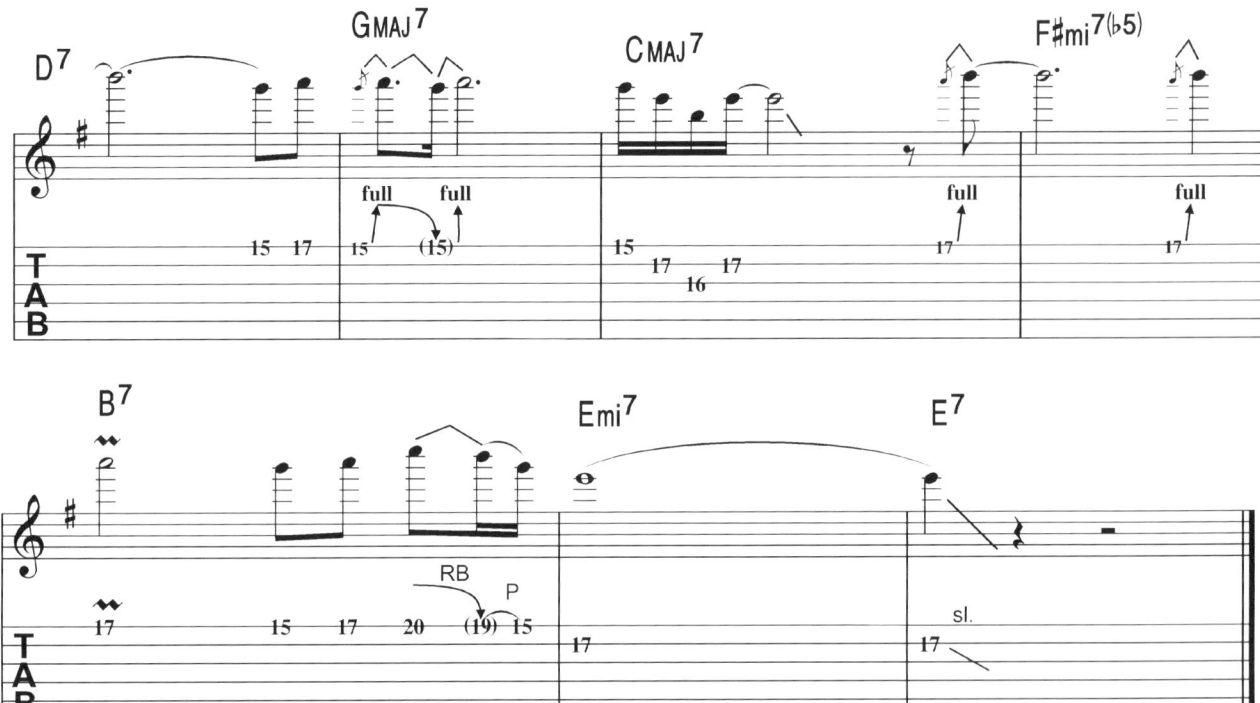

Here is a brief look at what was played.

1. Linking thirds of each chord.
2. Motif based on the first, second and third notes of each scale.
3. Linking thirds with chromaticism.
4. Bop clichés.
5. Repetitive licks using intervals of a fourth and unison.
6. Blues licks.

Thanks for checking this book out and I hope you'll have fun applying some of my ideas to your music.

Carl Filipiak